Mercier Press is the oldest independent Irish
publishing house and has published books in the
fields of history, literature, folklore, music, art,
humour, drama, politics, current affairs, law
and religion. It was founded in 1944 by John
and Mary Feehan.

In the building up of a country
few needs are as great as that of a publishing
house which would make the people proud of
their past, and proud of themselves as a people
capable of inspiring and supporting a world of
books which was their very own. Mercier Press
has tried to be that publishing house. On the
occasion of our fiftieth anniversary we thank
the many writers and readers who have
supported us and contributed to our success.

We face our second half-century
with confidence.

THE IRISH
LEPRECHAUN BOOK

Selected by
MARY FEEHAN

MERCIER PRESS

Mercier Press
PO Box 5, 5 French Church Street, Cork
24 Lower Abbey Street, Dublin 1

© Selection M. Feehan, 1994

A CIP record for this book is available from the British Library.

ISBN 1 85635 089 4

10   9   8   7   6   5   4   3   2   1

Printed in Ireland by Colour Books Ltd.

CONTENTS

Preface 7

1. Leprechauns and Cluricauns 9
   by Carolyn White
2. The Leprechaun 14
   by Lady Wilde
3: Seeing is Believing 21
   by T. Crofton Croker
4. The Leprechaun, or Fairy Shoemaker 26
   by William Allingham
5. The Little Shoe 29
   by T. Crofton Croker
6. The Shoemaker and Himself 32
   by Michael Scott
7. The Leprechaun 52
   by Robert Dwyer Joyce
8. The Field of Boliauns 54
   by T. Crofton Croker
8. Master and Man 59
   by T. Crofton Croker
10. The Big Man of the Fairies 69
   by Seumas O'Kelly

PREFACE

THE LEPRECHAUN IS the most famous, or in-
famous of all Irish fairies and T. Crofton Croker[*]
believed that the Cluricaun of the southern counties
of Ireland appears to be the same as the Leprechaun of Leinster.

The Leprechaun's main job is shoe-making and
according to Carolyn White[†] all the other fairies
tolerate him because after a few nights of dancing
even the strongest shoes wear out, and so the
services of the Leprechaun are essential.

He always carries a small purse with two coins
in it. One of these is magical – no matter how often
it is spent another takes its place. Because humans
discovered this secret the Leprechaun, if caught,
usually hands over the other coin and while the
human is examining the coin the Leprechaun
escapes.

Leprechauns are supposed to know the location
of buried treasure and they guard this secret very
closely. If you manage to catch one, then you must
hold him very firmly and never, even for one
second, take your eyes off him, because in the blink
of an eye he can disappear and he will use every
trick he knows to escape – so be warned!

---

[*] T. Crofton Croker, *Fairy Legends and Traditions of the South of Ireland.*
[†] Carolyn White, *A History of Irish Fairies.*

1: LEPRECHAUNS AND CLURICAUNS

CAROLYN WHITE[*]

THE LEPRECHAUN IS a solitary creature avoiding contact not only with mortals but with other Leprechauns, and, indeed, with the entire fairy tribe. He cannot endure their fickle frivolity nor they his dour manner. While trooping fairies delight in variegated experience, he pours all the passion of his concentrated soul into the careful making of shoes. A Leprechaun will always be found with a shoe in one hand and a hammer in the other.

All Leprechauns are ugly, stunted creatures, no taller than boys of ten or twelve, but broad and bulky, with faces like dried apples. But their eyes are always mischievously alight, and their bodies, despite their stubbiness, lithe. Leprechauns disappear behind trees faster than the mortal eye can follow.

And despite their possession of all the earth's treasure, they never sport clothes more elegant than drab, usually grey-coloured coats, sturdy leather

[*] From *A History of Irish Fairies* by Carolyn White

pocket-studded aprons and, for a bit of colour, dusty-red cocked hats.

Leprechauns are a querulous, sottish and foul-mouthed breed – the bane of the fairer fairylanders. They smoke ill-smelling stumps of pipes called dúidíns and guzzle intemperate draughts of beer from ever handy jugs. But the fairy gentry endure them because they provide the much needed service of cobblery. A few nights of intensive fairy dancing wear even the sturdiest of shoes; and so the Leprechauns must ply their trade assiduously to meet the fairy demand. Luckily, drinking never unsteadies the hand holding the hammer.

Leprechauns guard the fairies' treasure as well as shoe their feet. Not only must they prevent the theft of treasure by mortals, but they must avert its waste by their profligate trooping brethren. Trooping fairies do not understand the value of a ruby nor care to store for the future. They are lavish when they have, indifferent when they have not.

Without the Leprechauns as bankers, the fairies would centuries ago have squandered their fortune within and without their borders. Since treasure belongs to all fairies, any fairy can spend, much to the Leprechauns' chagrin, what he wills. And so although Leprechauns grumble, they begrudgingly give what is asked; for, in truth, Leprechauns live in awe of their fine-featured relatives.

Unlike the trooping fairies, the solitary fairies have a memory for the past. The trooping *sidhe* cannot keep abreast of short-lived mortal affairs; the solitary fairies never forget, but limit their interests.

Whereas the banshees recall great mortal deeds, Leprechauns (alone of the *sidhe*) remember when the marauding Danes landed in Ireland and where they hid their treasure. This memorable virtue, coupled with a remembrance of subsequent burials, gives Leprechauns the decided advantage in treasure-guarding.

Although Leprechauns bury their treasure well to keep it from profligate fairy and greedy mortal hands, rainbows frustrate their efforts by rudely settling themselves over particular gold hordes. By its presence a rainbow alerts mortals to a treasure's whereabouts, thereby causing the Guardian-Leprechaun incalculable anxiety. No matter how fast the little creature moves his pot, he never eludes the adherent rainbow. Luckily he usually manages to elude the grasp of the pursuant mortal, always baffled at the rainbow's inaccessibility.

If a mortal catches a Leprechaun (a possible task due to his absorption in treasure-counting and his frequent over-indulgence in drink), he must closely hold the little fellow, fixing an eye on him, and sternly demand his treasure. The Leprechaun never refuses. But only a rare man actually recovers the horde. Invariably the Leprechaun manages to turn the man's head – perhaps with a tale of his favourite horse's fall into the sinking bog – and, like a greased pig, slips from the tight grip. Once a man forced a Leprechaun to disclose a treasure buried beneath a tree. Tying a red scarf around the tree to mark it, the man then dashed home for a spade, having elicited from the Leprechaun an oath to touch neither scarf nor treasure. And neither did he. But when the man returned, every tree in the wood sported a red scarf.

Since mortals and fairies either avoid them or approach them to exact their gold, Leprechauns have become accustomed to trust only themselves. But kind acts sentimentally affect them and prompt them to respond in a generous manner. Sometimes in a moment of alcoholic geniality a Leprechaun offers a mortal not only a drink but some of his treasure, or a shilling contained in a leather purse having the property of perpetual replenishment. An impoverished nobleman who had given a wee fellow a lift on his horse found his dilapidated castle the next day stacked to its leaky ceiling with gold coins. Once a Leprechaun with a sentimental streak gave his treasure to a man claiming part-Leprechaun blood. And on an extraordinarily generous occasion one gave a golden bridle which, whenever shaken, produced a strong yellow steed attached to it.

Female Leprechauns do not exist; and since female fairies and mortals find the males physically repulsive, Leprechaun reproduction is doubtful. Leprechauns themselves are reticent about their births as they are secretive about most things. Perhaps they were the defective children of beautiful fairy parents who ejected them from the fairy troop because of their shape and disposition, but endured their separated existences as long as they cobbled shoes and guarded treasure.

Much debate has arisen as to whether Cluricauns are actually Leprechauns or degenerate close cousins. Save for a pink tinge about the nose, Cluricauns perfectly resemble Leprechauns in all their physical construction. But they never sport an apron or carry a hammer or manifest any desire to work. They look and act like weekend gentlemen: silver buckles adorn their shoes, gold laces their caps and pale blue stockings their stocky calves. They unabashedly enter rich men's wine cellars as if they were their own and drain the casks. For amusement they harness sheep and goats and shepherds' dogs, jump the bogs and race them over the fields through the night until the beasts are muddy and beaten with fatigue.

Leprechauns sternly declare these pleasure-seekers to be none of their own. Those believing their word argue that while extravagantly clothed Cluricauns tipple the wine glass, self-respecting Leprechauns in working dress drink nothing but beer. Yet since Cluricauns do act like working men putting on aristocratic airs, many suspect them to be nothing other than Leprechauns on a spree, who, in the sobering morning, haughtily deny a perverse double nature. The question remains insoluble because neither reckless drunkards nor creatures with reputations to preserve can be thoroughly trusted.

2:
THE LEPRECHAUN*

LADY WILDE†

THE LEPRECHAUNS ARE merry, industrious, tricksy little sprites, who do all the shoemaker's work and the tailor's and the cobbler's for the fairy gentry, and are often seen at sunset under the hedge singing and stitching. They know all the secrets of hidden treasure, and if they take a fancy to a person will guide him to the spot in the fairy rath where the pot of gold lies buried. It is believed that a family now living near Castlerea came by their riches in a strange way, all through the good offices of a friendly Leprechaun. And the legend has been handed down through many generations as an established fact.

There was a poor boy once, one of their forefathers, who used to drive his cart of turf daily back and forward, and make what money he could by the sale; but he was a strange boy, very silent and

---

* Leprechaun, or *Leith Brogan*, means the 'Artisan of the Brogue'.
† From *Ancient Legends, Mystic Charms and Superstitions of Ireland* by Lady Wilde.

moody, and the people said he was a fairy change-ling, for he joined in no sports and scarcely ever spoke to any one, but spent the nights reading all the old bits of books he picked up in his rambles. The one thing he longed for above all others was to get rich and to be able to give up the old weary turf cart, and live in peace and quietness all alone, with nothing but books round him, in a beautiful house and garden all by himself.

Now he had read in the old books how the Lep-rechauns knew all the secret places where gold lay hidden, and day by day he watched for a sight of the little cobbler, and listened for the click, click of his hammer as he sat under the hedge mending the shoes.

At last, one evening, just as the sun set, he saw a little fellow under a dock leaf, working away, dressed all in green, with a cocked hat on his head. So the boy jumped down from the cart and seized him by the neck.

'Now, you don't stir from this,' he cried, 'till you tell me where to find the hidden gold.'

'Easy now,' said the Leprechaun, 'don't hurt me, and I will tell you all about it. But mind you, I could hurt you if I chose, for I have the power; but I won't do it, for we are cousins once removed. So as we are near relations I'll just be good, and show you the place of the secret gold that none can have or keep except those of fairy blood and race. Come along with me, then, to the old fort of Lipenshaw, for there it lies. But make haste, for when the last red glow of the sun vanishes the gold will dis-

15

appear also, and you will never find it again.'

'Come off, then,' said the boy, and he carried the Leprechaun into the turf cart, and drove off. And in a second they were at the old fort, and went in through a door made in the stone wall.

'Now, look round,' said the Leprechaun, and the boy saw the whole ground covered with gold pieces, and there were vessels of silver lying about in such plenty that all the riches of all the world seemed gathered there.

'Now take what you want,' said the Leprechaun, 'but hasten, for if that door shuts you will never leave this place as long as you live.'

So the boy gathered up his arms full of gold and silver, and flung them into the cart; and was on his way back for more when the door shut with a clap like thunder, and all the place became dark as night. And he saw no more of the Leprechaun, and had not time even to thank him.

So he thought it best to drive home at once with his treasure, and when he arrived and was all alone by himself he counted his riches, and all the bright yellow gold pieces, enough for a king's ransom.

And he was very wise and told no one; but went off next day to Dublin and put all his treasures into the bank, and found that he was now indeed as rich as a lord.

So he ordered a fine house to be built with spacious gardens, and he had servants and carriages and books to his heart's content. And he gathered all the wise men round him to give him the learning of a gentleman; and he became a great and powerful man in the country, where his memory is still held in high honour, and his descendants are living to this day rich and prosperous; for their wealth has never decreased though they have ever given largely to the poor, and are noted above all things for the friendly heart and the liberal hand.

BUT THE LEPRECHAUNS can be bitterly malicious if they are offended, and one should be very cautious in dealing with them, and always treat them with great civility, or they will take revenge and never reveal the secret of the hidden gold.

One day a young lad was out in the fields at work when he saw a little fellow, not the height of his hand, mending shoes under a dock leaf. And he went over, never taking his eyes off him for fear he would vanish away; and when he got quite close he made a grab at the creature, and lifted him up and put him in his pocket.

Then he ran away home as fast as he could, and when he had the Leprechaun safe in the house, he tied him by an iron chain to the hob.

'Now, tell me,' he said, 'where am I to find a pot of gold? Let me know the place or I'll punish you.'

'I know of no pot of gold,' said the Leprechaun; 'but let me go that I may finish mending the shoes.'

'Then I'll make you tell me,' said the lad.

And with that he made down a great fire, and put the little fellow on it and scorched him.

'Oh, take me off, take me off!' cried the Leprechaun, 'and I'll tell you. Just there, under the dock

17

leaf, where you found me, there is a pot of gold. Go, dig and find.'

So the lad was delighted, and ran to the door; but it so happened that his mother was just then coming in with the pail of fresh milk, and in his haste he knocked the pail out of her hand, and all the milk was spilled on the floor.

Then, when the mother saw the Leprechaun, she grew very angry and beat him. 'Go away, you little wretch!' she cried. 'You have overlooked the milk and brought ill-luck.' And she kicked him out of the house.

But the lad ran off to find the dock leaf, though he came back very sorrowful in the evening, for he had dug and dug nearly down to the middle of the earth; but no pot of gold was to be seen.

That same night the husband was coming home from his work, and as he passed the old fort he heard voices and laughter; and one said, 'They are looking for a pot of gold; and they little know that a crock of gold is lying down in the bottom of the old quarry, hid under the stones close by the garden wall. But whoever gets it must go of a dark night at twelve o'clock, and beware of bringing his wife with him.'

So the man hurried home and told his wife he would go that very night, for it was black dark, and she must stay at home and watch for him, and not stir from the house till he came back. Then he went out into the dark night alone.

'Now,' thought the wife, when he was gone, 'if I could only get to the quarry before him I would have the pot of gold all to myself; while if he gets it I shall have nothing.'

And with that she went out and ran like the wind until she reached the quarry, and then she began to creep down very quietly in the black dark. But a great stone was in her path, and she stumbled over it, and fell down and down till she reached the bottom, and there she lay groaning, for her leg was broken by the fall.

Just then her husband came to the edge of the quarry and began to descend. But when he heard the groans he was frightened.

'Cross of Christ about us!' he exclaimed. 'What is that down below? Is it evil, or is it good?'

'Oh, come down, come down and help me!' cried the woman. 'It's your wife is here, and my leg is broken, and I'll die if you don't help me.'

'And is this my pot of gold?' exclaimed the poor man. 'Only my wife with a broken leg lying at the bottom of the quarry.'

And he was at his wits' end to know what to do, for the night was so dark he could not see a hand before him. So he roused up a neighbour, and between them they dragged up the poor woman and carried her home, and laid her on the bed half dead from fright, and it was many a day before she was able to get about as usual; indeed she limped all her life long, so that the people said the curse of the Leprechaun was on her.

But as to the pot of gold, from that day to this not one of the family, father or son, or any belonging to them, ever set eyes on it. However, the little

Leprechaun still sits under the dock leaf of the hedge and laughs at them as he mends the shoes with his little hammer – tick tack, tick tack – but they are afraid to touch him, for now they know he can take his revenge.

3: SEEING IS BELIEVING

*T. CROFTON CROKER**

THERE'S A SORT OF people whom every one must have met with some time or other; people that pretend to disbelieve what, in their hearts, they believe and are afraid of. Now Felix O'Driscoll was one of these. Felix was a rattling, rollicking, harum-scarum, devil-may-care sort of fellow, like – but that's neither here nor there: he was always talking one nonsense or another; and among the rest of his foolery, he pretended not to believe in the fairies, the Cluricauns, and the Phoocas; and he even sometimes had the impudence to affect to doubt of ghosts, that every body believes in, at any rate.

Yet some people used to wink and look knowing when Felix was boasting, for it was observed that he was very shy of passing the ford of Ahnamoe after nightfall; and that when he was once riding past the old church of Grenaugh in the dark, even though he had got enough of poitín into him to make any man stout, he made the horse trot

---

* From T. Crofton Croker, *Fairy Legends and Traditions of the South of Ireland*.

so that there was no keeping up with him; and every now and then he would throw a sharp look out over his left shoulder.

One night there was a parcel of people sitting drinking and talking together at Larry Reilly's public-house, and Felix was one of the party. He was, as usual, getting on with his talk about the fairies, and swearing that he did not believe there were any live things, barring men and beasts, and birds and fish, and such things as a body could see, and he went on talking in so profane a way of the 'good people', that some of the company grew timid, and began to cross themselves, not knowing what might happen, when an old woman called Moirna Hogaune, with a long blue cloak about her, who had been sitting in the chimney corner smoking her pipe without taking any share in the conversation, took the pipe out of her mouth, threw the ashes out of it, spat in the fire, and, turning round, looked Felix straight in the face.

'And so you don't believe there are such things as Cluricauns, don't you?' said she.

Felix looked rather daunted, but he said nothing.

'Upon my troth, it well becomes the like o' you, that's nothing but a bit of a garsún, to take upon you to pretend not to believe what your father and your father's father, and his father before him, ever made the least doubt of! But to make the matter short, seeing's believing, they say; and I that might be your grandmother tell you there are such things as Cluricauns, and I myself saw one – there's for

22

you, now!'

All the people in the room looked quite surprised at this, and crowded up to the fireplace to listen to her. Felix tried to laugh, but it wouldn't do; nobody minded him.

'I remember,' said she, 'some time after I married my honest man, who's now dead and gone, it was by the same token just a little before I lay in of my first child (and that's many a long day ago), I was sitting out in our bit of garden with my knitting in my hand, watching some bees that we had that were going to swarm. It was a fine sunshiny day about the middle of June, and the bees were humming and flying backwards and forwards from the hives, and the birds were chirping and hopping on the bushes, and the butterflies were flying about and sitting on the flowers, and every thing smelt so fresh, and so sweet, and I felt so happy, that I hardly knew where I was. When all of a sudden I heard, among some rows of beans that we had in a corner of the garden, a noise that went tick-tack, tick-tack, just for all the world as if a brogue-maker was putting on the heel of a pump. "Lord preserve us!" said I to myself. "What in the world can that be?"

'So I laid down my knitting, and got up and stole softly over to the beans, and never believe me if I did not see sitting there before me, in the middle of them, a bit of an old man not a quarter so big as a new-born child, with a little cocked hat on his head, and a dúidín in his mouth smoking away, and a plain old-fashioned drab-coloured coat with big buttons upon it on his back, and a pair of massy silver buckles in his shoes, that almost covered his feet, they were so big; and he working away as hard as ever he could, heeling a little pair of brogues.

'As soon, as I clapped my two eyes upon him, I knew him to be a Cluricaun; and as I was stout and foolhardy, says I to him, "God save you, honest man! That's hard work you're at this hot day."

'He looked up in my face quite vexed like; so with that I made a run at him, caught a hold of him in my hand, and asked him where was his purse of money.

'"Money?" said he, "Money, indeed! And where would a poor little old creature like me get money?"

'"Come, come," said I, "none of your tricks. Doesn't every body know that Cluricauns, like you, are as rich as the devil himself?"

'So I pulled out a knife I had in my pocket, and put on as wicked a face as ever I could (and, in troth, that was no easy matter for me then, for I was as comely and good-humoured a looking girl as you'd see from this to Carrignavar) and swore if he didn't instantly give me his purse, or show me a pot of gold, I'd cut the nose off his face.

'Well, to be sure, the little man did look so frightened at hearing these words, that I almost found it in my heart to pity the poor little creature. "Then," said he, "come with me just a couple of fields off, and I'll show you where I keep my money."

'So I went, still holding him in my hand and keeping my eyes fixed upon him, when all of a sudden I heard a whiz-z behind me.

'"There! there!" cried he. "There's your bees all swarming and going off with themselves."

'I, like a fool as I was, turned my head round, and when I saw nothing at all, and looked back at the Cluricaun, I found nothing at all at all in my hand, for when I had the ill luck to take my eyes off him, he slipped out of my hand just as if he was made of fog or smoke, and the sorrow the foot he ever came nigh my garden again.'

4: The Leprechaun, or Fairy Shoemaker (A Rhyme for Children)

William Allingham

LITTLE COWBOY, WHAT have you heard,
Up on the lonely rath's green mound?
Only the plaintive yellow-bird
Sighing in sultry fields around
Chary, Chary, Chary, chee-e!
Only the grasshopper and the bee?
'Tip-tap, rip-rap,
Tick-a-tack-too!
Scarlet leather sewn together,
This will make a shoe.
Left, right, pull it tight;
Summer days are warm;
Underground in winter,
Laughing at the storm!'
Lay your ear close to the hill:

Do you not catch the tiny clamour,
Busy click of an elfin hammer,
Voice of the Leprechaun singing shrill
As he merrily plies his trade?
He's a span
And a quarter in height.
Get him in sight, hold him tight,
And you're a made
Man!

You watch your cattle the summer day,
Sup on potatoes, sleep in the hay;
How would you like to roll in your carriage,
Look for a duchess' daughter in marriage?
Seize the shoemaker – then you may!
'Big boots a-hunting,
Sandals in the hall,
White for a wedding-feast,
Pink for a ball:
This way, that way,
So we make a shoe,
Getting rich every stitch,
Tick-tack-too!'
Nine-and-ninety treasure-crocks,
This keen miser-fairy hath,
Hid in mountains, woods, and rocks,
Ruin and round-tower, cave and rath,
And where the cormorants build;
From times of old
Guarded by him;
Each of them filled

Full to the brim
With gold!

I caught him at work one day, myself,
In the castle-ditch where foxglove grows –
A wrinkled, wizened, and bearded Elf,
Spectacles stuck on his pointed nose,
Silver buckles to his hose,
Leather apron, shoe in his lap –
'Rip-rap, tip-tap,
Tick-tack-too!
(A grig skipped upon my cap,
Away the moth flew!)
Buskins for a fairy prince,
Brogues for his son,
Pay me well, pay me well,
When the job is done!'
The rogue was mine, beyond a doubt.
I stared at him; he stared at me!
'Servant, Sir!' 'Humph!' says he,
And pulled a snuff-box out.
He took a long pinch, looked better pleased,
The queer little Leprechaun;
Offered the box with a whimsical grace –
Pouf! he flung the dust in my face –
And, while I sneezed,
Was gone!

5: THE LITTLE SHOE

T. CROFTON CROKER *

'NOW TELL ME, Molly,' said Mr Coote to Molly Cogan, as he met her on the road one day, close to one of the old gateways of Killmallock, 'did you ever hear of the Cluricaun?'

'Is it the Cluricaun? Why, then, sure I did, often and often; many's the time I heard my father, rest his soul! tell about 'em over and over again.'

'But did you ever see one, Molly – did you ever see one yourself?'

'Och! no, I never see one in my life; but my grandfather, that's my father's father, you know, he see one, one time, and caught him too.'

'Caught him! Oh! Molly, tell me how was that?'

'Why, then, I'll tell you. My grandfather, you see, was out there above in the bog, drawing home turf, and the poor old mare was tired after her day's work, and the old man went out to the stable to look after her, and to see if she was eating her hay; and when he came to the stable-door there, my

* From T. Crofton Croker, *Fairy Legends and Traditions of the South of Ireland.*

dear, he heard something hammering, hammering, hammering, just for all the world like a shoemaker making a shoe, and whistling all the time the prettiest tune he ever heard in his whole life before. Well, my grandfather, he thought it was the Cluricaun, and he said to himself, says he, "I'll catch you, if I can, and then I'll have money enough always."

'So he opened the door very quietly, and didn't make a bit of noise in the world that ever was heard; and he looked all about, but the never a bit of the little man he could see any where, but he heard him hammering and whistling, and so he looked and looked, till at last he see the little fellow; and where was he, do you think, but in the girth under the mare; and there he was with his little bit of an apron on him, and his hammer in his hand, and a little red nightcap on his head, and he making a shoe, and he was so busy with his work, and he was hammering and whistling so loud, that he never minded my grandfather till he caught him fast in his hand.

'"Faith, I have you now," says he, "and I'll never let you go till I get your purse – that's what I won't. So give it here to me at once, now."

'"Stop, stop," says the Cluricaun. "Stop, stop," says he, "till I get it for you."

'So my grandfather, like a fool, you see, opened his hand a little, and the little fellow jumped away laughing, and he never saw him any more, and the never a bit of the purse did he get, only the Cluricaun left his little shoe that he was making;

and my grandfather was mad enough angry with himself for letting him go; but he had the shoe all his life, and my own mother told me she often see it, and had it in her hand, and 'twas the prettiest little shoe she ever saw.'

'And did you see it yourself, Molly?'

'Oh! no, my dear, it was lost long before I was born; but my mother told me about it often and often enough.'

6: THE SHOEMAKER AND HIMSELF

MICHAEL SCOTT*

SEÁN LANE HAD always been a strange man, and from the moment he was born, people said that there was something amiss with him. He was small and dark with a sharp, pointed face and hard bright eyes. When he was a young boy, he would often stop and stare at something only he could see and then he would turn to his brother or sister and say, 'Did you not see the Leprechaun?' or 'That was one of the fairy folk.'

Of course, no one believed him. They all thought he was just a strange little boy, who used to tell lies. But the truth was that Seán could actually see the fairy folk – the *Sidhe*, and the Leprechauns and Cluricauns and *Fir Dearg* and once he even saw the terrible Banshee singing her terrifying lament outside a house to warn them of death.

When he grew up, Seán decided he would be a shoemaker. His own grandfather was a cobbler and would be able to teach him how to make and mend shoes and Seán – who was something of a lazy person – thought that cobbling would be an easy

* From *Irish Fairy Tales* by Michael Scott.

sort of a job. On summer days he would be able to sit outside his cottage, mending the shoes, and in winter he would be able to sit in front of a roaring fire. So, Seán went and lived with his grandfather for three years learning how to become a shoemaker, and in the end, when he thought he knew enough, he said goodbye to the old man and returned to his own village.

However, on his way home, Seán decided to take a short cut across the marsh. It was a dark and dreary place even on the hottest and brightest day, and the young shoemaker soon regretted his decision. The ground bubbled and steamed and swarms of flies and midges buzzed around his head. Once, he stumbled off the narrow path and sank ankle-deep into the thick, dirty water. He got such a fright that he decided to sit down and rest for a while before continuing across the marsh.

But the day was a hot one, and Seán soon fell asleep with his head resting against an ancient tree-stump. He awoke much later with a start, shivering with the evening chill. It took him a moment to realise where he was and then he wondered what had awakened him. He lay still and listened.

For a moment he heard nothing unusual, but then, faint and almost lost in the buzzing and sucking and creaking noises of the marsh, he heard a thin metallic plinking sound. Seán sat up and listened carefully. The noise sounded very familiar. He turned his head slightly towards the sound – and then he suddenly recognised it. It was the sound of a shoemaker's hammer hitting a nail.

But what would a shoemaker be doing in this part of the marsh?

The noise was coming from ahead of him, and Seán made up his mind to investigate. On hands and knees he crept down the path, heading towards the sound. The ringing noises grew louder as he neared it, and then Seán smelt the bitter-sweet odour of tobacco on the air. When the sound was coming from directly in front of him, Seán carefully raised his head and parted the thick blades of grass.

He found he was staring directly at a Leprechaun. The small man was sitting on a little mound of earth beneath the shade of a weeping willow tree, and Seán could see the black three-cornered hat, the dark green coat and the corners of his bright red stockings.

The young man could feel his heart beginning to pound. He had seen Leprechauns a few times before but only from the distance. They were very hard to catch, but if you managed to get hold of one and not take your eyes off him even for an instant, they would have to lead you to their hidden pots of gold. However, they had a hundred tricks for making sure they cheated you, and there were very many stories about the Little People escaping from the Big Folk – which was what they called humans. But this one would not get away, Seán promised. He took a deep breath and began to slide forward on the damp ground.

The Leprechaun should have heard the young man approaching, but it was a very hot day and he was tired and so he wasn't really paying attention to his surroundings. He heard nothing because he was tapping the shoe in his hand with his hammer and humming a little tune. So, he got a terrible fright when someone grabbed him by the shoulders and shouted, 'I've got you now, Mr Leprechaun, and you won't cheat me!'

The Leprechaun turned around and looked up at the Big Person. The Big Person, the Leprechaun decided, really wasn't such a big person after all; indeed, he was only a little bigger than himself.

Seán looked at the Leprechaun. Although he had the face and beard of an old man, his eyes were bright and lively, and he didn't really seem to be too worried about being caught.

'I've got you now,' Seán said, still holding the Leprechaun by the shoulders of his green coat.

'Aye, you have indeed,' the Leprechaun said quietly.

'I won't let you go.'

The Leprechaun shook his head. 'No, I didn't think you would. Now, tell me, what do you want from me?'

Seán was a little surprised. Why wasn't the Leprechaun frightened or angry at being captured?

'I suppose you want my crock of gold,' the Leprechaun continued. 'Well it won't work, because I haven't got one. I was captured last week by one of your people and I had to give up my gold then. And the Leprechaun can only have one pot of gold in a lifetime.'

'How do I know you're telling me the truth?' Seán demanded.

'Ah sure, why would I lie to you? The Little People never lie,' he said. 'They may not always tell the full truth, but they'll never tell you a lie.'

'Oh. So you've no gold?' the young man asked.

'Not so much as a gold button,' the Leprechaun said pleasantly.

'Nothing?' Seán asked. He was very disappointed; it was just his luck to get hold of a Leprechaun that someone else had caught before.

'Not so much as a silver sixpence.'

'Nothing?' he asked again.

'Not so much as a copper penny.'

'Well what do you have?' Seán demanded. 'I can't just let you go now, can I?'

The old man tilted his head to one side and considered.

'No, I don't suppose you can. It wouldn't really be right if you just let me go. Why, what would the other Little Folk say if they knew that I was caught and then just let go. No,' he said again, 'I'll either have to escape or pay you.'

'Well you won't escape,' Seán said. 'You see, I've a little of the fairy blood in me. I'm what the country people call fey. I can see the *sidhe* and the fairies – so you won't be able to escape that way.'

'Ah well then,' the Leprechaun said, 'I'll pay you for my freedom.'

'But if you've neither gold, silver nor copper how can you pay me?'

'With this!' The Leprechaun wriggled one hand free and pulled a small leather bag off his shoulder. 'I'll give you this!'

Seán, with one hand still holding tightly onto the Little Fellow, took the bag in his free hand. It was a small square leather bag with a strap to go around the shoulder. He opened it, but it was empty inside. However, he didn't refuse the gift just yet. This was a Leprechaun's bag and might just be magical.

When he had examined the bag carefully, he asked, 'What's so special about the bag?'

The Leprechaun smiled crookedly. 'Well now, I'll tell you. This might just look like a small black bag to you now – but this bag grows! You could put a table and four chairs in here and still have space for more.'

The young man looked at the bag again, and then back to the Leprechaun. 'You're sure now?' he said doubtfully.

'Sure I'm sure. And it's a bag that will never wear out or tear,' he added.

'A fine bag altogether,' Seán agreed, 'if what you're telling me is the truth.'

'Well, you'll just have to take my word for it,' the Leprechaun said.

Seán nodded. 'I suppose I will ...' And then he suddenly shook open the bag and popped it over the Leprechaun's head. Now the bag was so small that it should only have covered his head, but it grew ... and grew ... until the small man was completely inside it.

'Do you believe me now?' the Leprechaun asked in a muffled voice.

Seán stood back and looked at the bag with its

wriggling contents. It would be very handy to have a bag like that, he thought. He knelt down and unsnapped the little catches and shook the Leprechaun out. 'I believe you,' he said. 'I'll take the bag in exchange for your freedom.'

The little man stood up and dusted off his clothes and straightened his cap on his head. 'Aye, it's a good bag. You better be off now,' he said. 'It's getting late and you don't want to be trapped on the marsh at night.'

Seán looked up into the sky which was already beginning to darken in the east. The first of the night stars were beginning to peep through. He shivered as a cold breeze whistled through the lonely trees. 'No,' he agreed, 'what we really need is someone with a lantern to lead us across these marshes at night.'

The Leprechaun looked at him strangely for a moment. 'Aye, that we do.' He nodded, gave a short little bow, turned – and was gone!

Seán stood for a moment, wondering if he had been dreaming it all – but he did have the small black bag in his hand as proof. He slung it over his shoulder, pulled his coat tighter around his shoulders and set off as quickly as possible for home.

NOW THE YEARS passed. Some years were good for Seán, and he sold and mended a lot of shoes and made enough money to live well – but others were very bad, and he was forced to borrow food and money from his friends. Strangely, because Seán was such a good shoemaker, it helped to keep him poor. It took a long time for his shoes to wear out or need mending and so the people didn't have to go to him as often as they would with an ordinary pair of shoes or boots.

There was one very bad winter when he earned practically nothing. The weather was warm and dry, there was little frost and no snow, and no one needed their boots or shoes mended and so for three whole months he had no work. He began to borrow – just a little at first, but soon more and more. In a very short time he owed a lot of money. And soon those he had borrowed from began to get impatient as spring was approaching and they needed the money to buy crops and seed. But Seán had no money.

It was a bright, though cold February morning and he was sitting on the step outside his little cottage mending his own shoes when he saw the stranger approaching. He was a tall, thin dark man, dressed in a black overcoat, black trousers, shiny black shoes and a black hat. He was smoking a thin black cigar, and the smell of the tobacco was sharp and bitter on the fresh morning air. The stranger stopped at the gate.

'I'm looking for Seán Lane,' he said pleasantly. He spoke Irish with a strange foreign accent, and as he leaned across the gatepost, Seán noticed that he wore black gloves, but with a thick gold ring outside the glove on his little finger.

'I am Seán Lane,' the cobbler said, nodding courteously. 'What can I so for you, sir?'

The stranger smiled and pushed open the gate.

'Ah, but it's not what you can do for me, it's what I can do for you,' he said. He had a thin sort of smile which curled his lips but didn't brighten his eyes.

'I'm not sure I understand you,' Seán said.

The stranger stood before the shoemaker with his hands held behind his back. He was very tall and Seán had to lean back to look up at him. 'It has come to my notice that you are ...' he paused, and smiled again. 'Well, it seems you are a little short of money at present ...'

'Ach no,' Seán said quickly, beginning to get nervous now. 'I owe a few pounds here and there, that's all. But business is picking up, I'll soon be able to pay it all back.' He stood up. 'You know my name, sir, but I'm not sure that you told me yours.'

'I didn't,' the stranger said. 'But some people call me Himself.'

'Himself?'

'Yes,' the tall man smiled again. 'Have you never heard people say, "... it's himself that's coming now ..." or "... it was himself did this ...?"'

Seán nodded doubtfully. It was a common phrase used by the country people, but he had never thought that they were talking about a real person.

'Now,' Himself said, 'I've come to make a little bargain with you.'

'What sort of bargain?' Seán asked quickly.

'A small sort of one.'

'What are you offering me?'

'I'm offering you money – a lot of money – and the promise of a lot of business, as much as you can

40

handle. When I'm finished, you'll be the best known shoemaker in all Ireland.'

'And what's it going to cost me?' the shoemaker asked doubtfully.

'Only a promise.'

'What's the promise?'

Himself leaned forward until his face was only a few inches away from Seán's. His eyes looked very red. 'The promise is that you will come with me in seven years time. You won't ask any questions either,' he added.

'Where will I go?'

The stranger raised one long thin finger. 'No questions.'

Seán leaned back against the whitewashed wall of his cottage and thought about it. It was a very tempting offer; a lot a money and as much business as he could handle. He wasn't too sure about the other part of the deal though. And he had just a hint of an idea whom the stranger might be. He looked up at Himself. 'Can I think about this offer of yours?' he asked.

The tall man shook his head. 'This is an offer I make to very few people and I only make it once. I'm afraid you must make up your mind now. I've a train to catch to Dublin shortly.'

Seán came to a decision. 'Right then, I'll do it.'

Himself smiled in a very strange way. 'Excellent.' He reached inside his coat and pulled out a wad of notes and handed it to the shoemaker. 'Here you are. And I'll make sure you never want for business,' he added. The stranger then turned up the collar of his coat and settled his hat on his head. 'I'll be off now – but I'll see you in seven years time,' he added, his voice sounding like a warning. He nodded once and, before Seán could say anything else, he turned on his heel and walked away quickly, leaving the shoemaker alone with a handful of money.

The seven years seemed to pass very quickly for Seán Lane. As the stranger had promised, his business increased and he soon became famous as the best shoemaker in all Ireland. He moved from his little cottage to a bigger house and soon took on some apprentices. He even started seeing a girl from the nearby town, and he was just about beginning to think about asking her father for permission to marry her when he realised that the seven years were up.

It was a bitterly cold February morning when the stranger returned. Seán had just hopped out of bed and was splashing cold water on his face when he heard the front door bell ring. He stopped. It was only half-past seven, who could be calling so early in the morning? He crept to his bedroom door, put his ear against it and listened.

Downstairs, one of the young maids hurried to open the door. The shoemaker was the only man in the town who could afford to keep servants. The young girl opened the door and then jumped in fright at the figure who stood on the doorstep.

The tall thin man bowed slightly. 'Is this the Lane household?' he asked, first in Irish and then in English, in a strange, foreign-sounding accent.

'It is, sir,' she answered quietly.

'And is Mr Lane at home?' the man asked with a smile.

'He is, sir,' the maid answered. She stepped back and allowed the stranger to come into the hall. 'What name shall I give him?' she asked.

The tall foreigner smiled again. 'Oh, just say it's Himself.'

The maid hurried upstairs and tapped gently on the shoemaker's door. 'Sir ...?'

Seán hurried around the room, getting dressed. Seven years had certainly passed very quickly, although he had to admit that everything the stranger had promised had come true. Which meant that the stranger could only be ... the Devil Himself!

The shoemaker smiled then. He had partially guessed his identity seven years ago, and he had only accepted his deal because he had an idea how he might cheat the Devil. Seán Lane smiled again, picked up his magical Leprechaun's bag and opened the door.

Himself was waiting at the bottom of the stairs. In the seven years the stranger hadn't changed in the slightest. He even wore the same clothes he had worn then.

'Your time is up,' he said with a smile. 'You have to come with me now.'

Seán nodded. 'I've been expecting you. My bag is packed, and I've everything here that I'll need.'

'I don't think you'll need anything where you're going,' Himself said with a grin.

'Where I go, my bag goes with me,' Seán insisted.

'What's in the bag then?' the stranger asked.

'Oh, I couldn't tell you. A lot of things.'

'You couldn't fit a lot of things into that bag,' Himself said in a mocking voice.

'It holds enough for me,' the shoemaker said.

'Let me see then.'

'No.'

'But it won't hurt to let me see, now will it?' Himself asked.

'Well ...' Seán shrugged. 'Oh, I suppose it won't.' He knelt on the bottom step and opened the bag. The stranger knelt down beside him. He peeped into the bag.

'It's empty!' he said.

'It is not,' the shoemaker insisted.

Himself pointed. 'Look for yourself; there's nothing in it.'

'There is,' Seán persisted. 'Look.'

The stranger leaned over and peered closely into the bag – and Seán quickly pulled it up over his head. The bag grew ... and grew ... and grew ... and Seán snapped it shut on the tall thin stranger!

Seán danced a little jig on the bottom step beside the wriggling bag. 'I have you now, and you won't get out until you give back my promise.'

There was a muffled shout from inside the bag, and it sounded like 'No.' Seán heaved the long bag up onto his shoulder and set off towards the nearby town. The priest there might be able to help him, he thought.

But on his way into town he passed Farmer O'Neill's barn where the farmer and his two sons were threshing corn with flails, which were like small whips.

'A good-morning to you, Mr O'Neill,' he said, stopping by the door, resting his bag on the ground by his feet.

The farmer and his two sons stopped and nodded to the shoemaker. 'You're up early this morning, Mr Lane,' the old farmer said.

'Oh, I think today will be a busy day for me – and for you too, I see,' he said, pointing to the corn.

The farmer nodded, 'Aye, we've a lot to do.' He stopped and pointed to the bag. 'What have you got there, if you don't mind my asking?'

'A bag full of leather,' the shoemaker said, 'but it's very hard and I'm taking it into town to get it softened.'

'And how will you get it softened?' the farmer asked.

'Oh, I'll have it beaten for a while; that'll soften it up.'

'Beaten is it? Well now, if you give it here, the two lads and myself will beat it for you.'

'That's very kind of you,' Seán said, handing the black bag to the farmer.

'Will we take it out of the bag for you?' one of the farmer's son's asked, reaching for the lock.

'No, no,' Seán said quickly. 'If you take the leather out of the bag the ... flails might mark and tear the surface,' he said, saying the first thing that came into his mind.

Mr O'Neill nodded. 'Of course. Well then, we'll just beat the whole lot – bag and all. Stand back now,' he warned. Then the farmer and his two sons began to beat the bag with all their might. They pounded on it for one full hour and when they were finished the black bag was soft and limp. The old farmer handed it back to the shoemaker. 'There you are, I hope that's a little better.'

'It is indeed,' Seán said with a big grin. 'Thank you very much for all your trouble.' He heaved the bag over his shoulder and, waving the O'Neill's goodbye, continued on down the road towards the town.

A little further on, Seán came to the Tully Brother's Foundry. The three Tully brothers were blacksmiths, and when the shoemaker arrived, they were busy making and shaping horse-shoes.

One was pumping the bellows to blow air into the fire, making the coals glow white-hot, and the other two were using their heavy hammers to twist thin bars of metal into half circles, which would then be shaped into shoes.

They stopped when they saw Seán passing and wished him a good morning.

'A good-morning to you,' Seán said. 'How are those new shoes I made you a while ago?' he asked Gerard, the oldest and largest of the three brothers.

'They fit like a glove,' the huge man said, 'like a glove. Now, remember what I said to you then, if there's anything I can do for you in return ...'

'Well,' Seán said, 'there is something ...'

'You just name it,' Gerard said, rubbing his

hands on his thick leather apron and leaning on his hammer.

'This is a bag full of leather which I'm taking into town to be softened,' Seán said, holding up the black bag, 'but I was wondering if you could just beat on it for a while – just to help soften it up, you know.'

'Will we not tear the bag?' Gerard wondered.

'Not this bag,' Seán promised. 'It's stronger than it looks.'

So the three Tully brothers took it in turns to beat the bag with their hammers. Each one hammered it for an hour and at the end of three hours they were surprised to find it was still in one piece.

'That's a fine bag you have there,' Gerard said to Seán, handing it back to him. 'If you should ever think of selling it, come to me.'

'Oh, I couldn't sell this,' Seán said, 'I've had it for years, it's very special.' He thanked the three blacksmiths and then waved goodbye.

It was now close to mid-morning and he had one last stop to make before he had a few more words with Himself.

The shoemaker's final stop was at Devaney's Mill on the hill above the town. Old Mr Devaney had been the miller for nearly forty years. He made all the bread for the town and some for the nearby villages, and his mill was the largest and most famous in the county on account of its huge grinding stones.

Seán made his way up the hill and went in through the always-open door into the back of the mill where the flour was ground. The old miller saw him and waved.

'A good-morning to you, Mr Lane, and what brings you up here? Is it freshly-baked, warm bread you're looking for, eh?'

Seán smiled. Devaney's bread was delicious, and his favourite. 'Oh, I'll have some of your bread Mr Devaney, but I've come to ask a favour of you.'

The white-haired old man smiled broadly. 'Ask away.'

The shoemaker held up the black bag. 'Would you put this bag of mine on your mill, and let it turn for a little while?'

'But that will destroy your bag,' the old man protested.

The shoemaker shook his head. 'Oh, no, this is a stronger bag than it looks.'

'Well if you say so ...' Mr Devaney said doubtfully. He took the black bag and put it on the wheel and then the huge mill stone came around and crushed it flat against the second stone. The huge stone rumbled away and then came around again and again and again ...

An hour later, Mr Devaney gave the bag back to Seán. 'I'm surprised it's not in shreds,' he said.

'I told you it was a special sort of bag.' He thanked the old miller and set off for home, munching on a warm loaf of bread.

When he returned to his own house, he went out to the barn and set the bag on the ground. He leaned close to it and said, 'I'll let you out if our deal is off. Promise.'

THE IRISH LEPRECHAUN BOOK

There was a long pause and then the Devil said faintly, 'I promise.'

Seán opened the bag and shook Himself out. The Devil looked very battered and bedraggled, and his fine black clothes were covered with white flour. He got to his feet and shook his fist at the shoemaker. 'You're a terrible man. I don't think I would want you as a devil,' he snapped and then he closed his eyes and disappeared in a crack of blue fire.

The shoemaker leaned back and laughed for a long, long time. He had cheated the Devil.

SEÁN LIVED TO be a very old man, and he was nearly ninety years old before he died. And of course he went straight to Hell – for he had sold his soul to the Devil, even if Himself wouldn't take it! The door to Hell was made from black marble with large silver bolts set into it and a huge silver knocker in the shape of a dragon's head set in the centre of it. Seán took hold of it and knocked loudly.

For a long time nothing happened and then, slowly, very slowly, the door creaked open. There was no one there. 'Yes?' a voice suddenly asked, booming and echoing as if it came from a great distance.

'Well,' Seán said, 'I've just died, and I've ended up here, so I suppose this is where I've got to come.'

A figure stepped into the doorway. It was the tall thin, dark-faced man with sharp eyes. He wasn't dressed all in black this time, but Seán recognised him.

'Ah, it's yourself,' he smiled.

The Devil started and then looked closely at the man standing on the doorstep. 'You!' He stepped back and shook his head. 'You're not coming in here; I remember what you did to me the last time.'

'Well, where will I go then?' Seán asked.

'You can try the Other Place,' the Devil said and, stepping back, he slammed the door shut.

Seán turned his back on Hell and set off along the road of black marble, returning the way he had come. Soon the colour of the road changed to grey and then to white and he soon saw the white marble gate of Heaven in the distance.

It looked very like the gate of Hell, except that this was all white marble and with gold bolts and studs. It had a gold knocker made in the shape of a smiling angel. Seán took hold of the knocker and gently rapped on the door.

The door was opened almost immediately by a tall, thin figure dressed all in white. Seán tried to see over his shoulders, but he couldn't see any signs of wings. 'Well?' the angel asked pleasantly.

'Well,' Seán began, 'I've just died and although I thought I had to go to Hell, Himself won't take me in.'

'Oh.' The angel looked very surprised. 'What's your name? I'll have to check my books.'

'Séan Lane, shoemaker,' he said.

The angel disappeared for a moment and when he returned he was holding a huge leather-bound book with gold clasps on the corners. He opened the book about half-way and ran his long thin finger down the heavy pages. 'Lane ... Lane ... yes, yes, here we are.' He read a few lines and then looked down at the shoemaker. 'Sold your soul to Himself, did you? Well, we cannot have you here.'

'But he won't have me down there,' Seán protested. 'What am I going to do?'

The angel considered for a moment, and then he read some more of the shoemaker's life. Finally, he looked up and smiled. 'We'll have to send you back,' he said.

'Back?'

'Yes, back down to Earth. We'll give you a penance to do, and maybe in a few hundred years you'll be able to come in here.'

Seán nodded. 'What do I have to do then?'

The angel tapped the page with his finger. 'It says here that you once said that there should be someone with a light to lead people across dangerous marshes at night.

'Did I say that?' Seán asked, and then he remembered. It has been that day he had been give the black bag by the Leprechaun. 'I remember it now.'

The angel closed the book with a thump. 'Well then – that's what you'll do ...'

It is said that Seán wanders this world still. You can see him sometimes as he roams across the marshes with his lantern. The country people call his spirit, Jack o' the Lantern ...

7: THE LEPRECHAUN

ROBERT DWYER JOYCE

IN A SHADY nook one moonlit night,
   A leprechaun I spied
In scarlet coat and cap of green,
   A cruiskeen by his side.
'Twas tick, tack, tick, his hammer went,
   Upon a weeny shoe,
And I laughed to think of a purse of gold,
   But the fairy was laughing too.

With tip-toe step and beating heart,
   Quite softly I drew nigh.
There was mischief in his merry face,
   A twinkle in his eye;
He hammered and sang with tiny voice,
   And sipped the mountain dew;
Oh! I laughed to think he was caught at last,
   But the fairy was laughing, too.

As quick as thought I grasped the elf,
   'Your fairy purse,' I cried,
'My purse?' said he, "tis in her hand,

That lady by your side.'
I turned to look, the elf was off,
And what was I to do?
Oh! I laughed to think what a fool I'd been,
And, the fairy was laughing too.

8: THE FIELD OF BOLIAUNS

T. CROFTON CROKER*

TOM FITZPATRICK WAS the eldest son of a comfortable farmer who lived at Ballincollig. Tom was just turned of nine-and-twenty, when he met the following adventure, and was as clever, clean, tight, good-looking a boy as any in the whole county Cork. One fine day in harvest – it was indeed Lady-day in harvest, that every body knows to be one of the greatest holidays in the year – Tom was taking a ramble through the ground, and went sauntering along the sunny side of a hedge, thinking in himself, where would be the great harm if people, instead of idling and going about doing nothing at all, were to shake out the hay, and bind and stook the oats that were lying on the ledge, 'specially as the weather had been rather broken of late, he all of a sudden heard a clacking sort of noise a little before him, in the hedge.

'Dear me,' said Tom, 'but isn't it surprising to hear the stone-chatters singing so late in the

---

* From T. Crofton Croker, *Fairy Legends and Traditions of the South of Ireland*.

season?'

So Tom stole on, going on the tops of his toes to try if he could get a sight of what was making the noise, to see if he was right in his guess. The noise stopped; but as Tom looked sharply through the bushes, what should he see in a nook of the hedge but a brown pitcher that might hold about a gallon and a half of liquor; and by and by a little wee diny dony bit of an old man, with a little *motty* of a cocked hat stuck upon the top of his head, and a deeshy daushy leather apron hanging before him, pulled out a little wooden stool, and stood up upon it and dipped a little piggin into the pitcher, and took out the full of it, and put it beside the stool, and then sat down under the pitcher, and began to work at putting a heel-piece on a bit of a brogue just fitting for himself.

'Well, by the powers!' said Tom to himself. 'I often heard tell of the Cluricaun; and, to tell God's truth, I never rightly believed in them – but here's one of them in real earnest. If I go knowingly to work, I'm a made man. They say a body must never take their eyes off them, or they'll escape.'

Tom now stole on a little farther, with his eye fixed on the little man just as a cat does with a mouse, or, as we read in books, the rattle-snake does with the birds he wants to enchant. So when he got up quite close to him, 'God bless your work, neighbour,' said Tom.

The little man raised up his head, and, 'Thank you kindly,' said he.

'I wonder you'd be working on the holy-day?'

said Tom.

'That's my own business, not yours,' was the reply.

'Well, may be you'd be civil enough to tell us what you've got in the pitcher there?' said Tom.

'That I will, with pleasure,' said he. 'It's good beer.'

'Beer!' said Tom. 'Thunder and fire! Where did you get it?'

'Where did I get it, is it? Why, I made it. And what do you think I made it of?'

'Devil a one of me knows,' said Tom, 'but of malt, I suppose. What else?'

'There you're out. I made it of heath.'

'Of heath!' said Tom, bursting out laughing. 'Sure you don't think me to be such a fool as to believe that?'

'Do as you please,' said he, ' but what I tell you is the truth. Did you never hear tell of the Danes?'

'And that I did,' said Tom. 'Weren't them the fellows we gave such a licking when they thought to take Limerick from us?'

'Hem!' said the little man drily. 'Is that all you know about the matter?'

'Well, but about them Danes?' said Tom.

'Why, all the about them there is, is that when they were here they taught us to make beer out of the heath, and the secret's in my family ever since.'

'Will you give a body a taste of your beer?' said Tom.

'I'll tell you what it is, young man – it would be fitter for you to be looking after your father's property than to be bothering decent, quiet people with your foolish questions. There now, while you're idling away your time here, the cows have broke into the oats, and are knocking the corn all about.'

Tom was taken so by surprise with this, that he was just on the very point of turning round when he recollected himself; so, afraid that the like might happen again, he made a grab at the Cluricaun and caught him up in his hand; but in his hurry he overset the pitcher, and spilt all the beer, so that he could not get a taste of it to tell what sort it was. He then swore what he would not do to him if he did not show him where his money was. Tom looked so wicked and so bloody-minded, that the little man was quite frightened; so, says he, 'Come along with me a couple of fields off, and I'll show you a crock of gold.'

So they went, and Tom held the Cluricaun fast in his hand, and never took his eyes off him, though they had to cross hedges, and ditches, and a crooked bit of bog (for the Cluricaun seemed, out of pure mischief, to pick out the hardest and most contrary way), till at last they came to a great field all full of boliaun buies (ragweed), and the Cluricaun pointed to a big boliaun, and, says he, 'Dig under that boliaun, and you'll get the great crock all full of guineas.'

Tom in his hurry had never minded bringing a spade with him, so he thought to run home and fetch one; and that he might know the place again, he took off one of his red garters, and tied it round the boliaun.

'I suppose,' said the Cluricaun, very civilly, 'you've no farther occasion for me?'

'No,' says Tom. 'You may go away now, if you please, and God speed you, and may good luck attend you wherever you go.'

'Well, goodbye to you, Tom Fitzpatrick,' said the Cluricaun, 'and much good may do you, with what you'll get.'

So Tom ran, for the dear life, till he came home, and got a spade, and then away with him, as hard as he could go, back to the field of boliauns; but when he got there, lo, and behold! not a boliaun in the field but had a red garter, the very identical model of his own, tied about it; and as to digging up the whole field, that was all nonsense, for there was more than forty good Irish acres in it. So Tom came home again with his spade on his shoulder, a little cooler than he went; and many's the hearty curse he gave the Cluricaun every time he thought of the neat turn he had served him.

9: MASTER AND MAN

T. CROFTON CROKER*

BILLY MAC DANIEL was once as likely a young man as ever shook his brogue at a pattern, emptied a quart, or handled a shillelagh; fearing for nothing but the want of drink; caring for nothing but who should pay for it; and thinking of nothing but how to make fun over it: drunk or sober, a word and a blow was ever the way with Billy Mac Daniel; and a mighty easy way it is of either getting into, or of ending, a dispute. More is the pity that, through the means of his thinking, and fearing, and caring for nothing, this same Billy Mac Daniel fell into bad company; for surely the good people are the worst of all company any one could come across.

It so happened, that Billy was going home one clear frosty night not long after Christmas; the moon was round and bright; but although it was as fine a night as a heart could wish for, he felt pinched with the cold. 'By my word,' chattered Billy, 'a drop of good liquor would be no bad thing

---

* From T. Crofton Croker, *Fairy Legends and Traditions of the South of Ireland.*

to keep a man's soul from freezing in him; and I wish I had a full measure of the best.'

'Never wish it twice, Billy,' said a little man in a three-cornered hat, bound all about with gold lace, and with great silver buckles in his shoes, so big that it was a wonder how he could carry them; and he held out a glass as big as himself, filled with as good liquor as ever eye looked on or lip tasted.

'Success, my little fellow,' said Billy Mac Daniel, nothing daunted, though well he knew the little man to belong to the *good people*; 'here's your health, anyway, and thank you kindly; no matter who pays for the drink'; and he took the glass and drained it to the very bottom, without ever taking a second breath to it.

'Success,' said the little man; 'and you're heartily welcome, Billy; but don't think to cheat me as you have done others – out with your purse and pay me like a gentleman.'

'Is it I pay you?' said Billy. 'Could I not just take you up and put you in my pocket as easily as a blackberry?'

'Billy Mac Daniel,' said the little man, getting very angry, 'you shall be my servant for seven years and a day, and that is the way I will be paid; so make ready to follow me.'

When Billy heard this, he began to be very sorry for having used such bold words towards the little man; and he felt himself, yet could not tell how, obliged to follow the little man the livelong night about the country, up and down, and over hedge and ditch, and through bog and brake without any rest.

When morning began to dawn, the little man turned round to him and said, 'You may now go home, Billy, but on your peril don't fail to meet me in the Fort-field tonight; or if you do, it may be the worse for you in the long run. If I find you a good servant, you will find me an indulgent master.'

Home went Billy Mac Daniel; and though he was tired and weary enough, never a wink of sleep could he get for thinking of the little man; but he was afraid not to do his bidding, so up he got in the evening, and away he went to the Fort-field. He was not long there before the little man came towards him and said, 'Billy, I want to go a long journey tonight; so saddle one of my horses, and you may saddle another for yourself, as you are to go along with me, and may be tired after your walk last night.'

Billy thought this very considerate of his master, and thanked him accordingly: 'But,' said he, 'if I may be so bold, sir, I would ask which is the way to your stable, for never a thing do I see but the Fort here, and the old thorn-tree in the corner of the field, and the stream running at the bottom of the hill, with the bit of bog over against us.'

'Ask no questions, Billy,' said the little man, 'but go over to that bit of bog, and bring me two of the strongest rushes you can find.'

Billy did accordingly, wondering what the little man would be at; and he picked out two of the stoutest rushes he could find, with a little bunch of brown blossom stuck at the side of each, and brought them back to his master.

'Get up, Billy,' said the little man, taking one of the rushes from him, and striding across it.

'Where shall I get up, please your honour?' said Billy.

'Why, upon horseback, like me, to be sure,' said the little man.

'Is it after making a fool of me you'd be,' said Billy, 'bidding me get a-horseback upon that bit of a rush? Maybe you want to persuade me that the rush I pulled but while ago out of the bog over there is a horse?'

'Up! up! and no words,' said the little man, looking very angry. 'The best horse you ever rode was but a fool to it.' So Billy, thinking all this was in joke, and fearing to vex his master, straddled across the rush. 'Borram! Borram! Borram!' cried the little man three times (which, in English, means to become great), and Billy did the same after him: presently the rushes swelled up into fine horses, and away they went full speed; but Billy, who put the rush between his legs, without much minding how he did it, found himself sitting on horseback the wrong way, which was rather awkward, with his face to the horse's tail; and so quickly had his steed started off with him, that he had no power to turn round, and there was therefore nothing for it but to hold on by the tail.

At last they came to their journey's end, and stopped at the gate of a fine house. 'Now, Billy,' said the little man, 'do as you see me do, and follow me close; but as you did not know your horse's

head from his tail, mind that your own head does
not spin round until you can't tell whether you are
standing on it or on your heels; for remember that
old liquor, though able to make a cat speak, can
make a man dumb.'

The little man then said some queer kind of
words, out of which Billy could make no meaning;
but he contrived to say them after him for all that;
and in they both went through the key-hole of the
door, and through one key-hole after another, until
they got into the wine-cellar, which was well stored
with all kinds of wine.

The little man fell to drinking as hard as he
could, and Billy, nowise disliking the example, did
the same. 'The best of masters are you, surely,' said
Billy to him. 'No matter who is the next; and well
pleased will I be with your service if you continue
to give me plenty to drink.'

'I have made no bargain with you,' said the
little man, 'and will make none; but up and follow
me.'

Away they went, through key-hole after key-
hole; and each mounting upon the rush which he
left at the hall door, scampered off, kicking the
clouds before them like snow-balls, as soon as the
word, 'Borram, Borram, Borram' had passed their
lips.

When they came back to the Fort-field, the little
man dismissed Billy, bidding him to be there the
next night at the same hour. Thus did they go on,
night after night, shaping their course one night
here, and another night there – sometimes north,

and sometimes east, and sometimes south, until there was not a gentleman's wine-cellar in all Ireland they had not visited, and could tell the flavour of every wine in it as well – ay, better, than the butler himself.

One night when Billy Mac Daniel met the little man as usual in the Fort-field, and was going to the bog to fetch the horses for their journey, his master said to him, 'Billy, I shall want another horse to-night, for maybe we may bring back more company with us than we take.'

So Billy, who now knew better than to question any order given to him by his master, brought a third rush, much wondering who it might be that would travel back in their company, and whether he was about to have a fellow-servant. 'If I have,' thought Billy, 'he shall go and fetch the horses from the bog every night; for I don't see why I am not, every inch of me, as good a gentleman as my master.'

Well, away they went, Billy leading the third horse, and never stopped until they came to a snug farmer's house in the county Limerick, close under the old castle of Carrigogunniel, that was built, they say, by the great Brian Boru. Within the house there was great carousing going forward, and the little man stopped outside for some time to listen; then turning round all of a sudden, said, 'Billy, I will be a thousand years old tomorrow!'

'God bless us, sir,' said Billy, 'will you!'

'Don't say these words again, Billy,' said the little man, 'or you will be my ruin for ever. Now,

Billy, as I will be a thousand years in the world tomorrow, I think it is full time for me to get married.'

'I think so too, without any kind of doubt at all,' said Billy, 'if ever you mean to marry.'

'And to that purpose,' said the little man, 'have I come all the way to Carrigogunniel; for in this house, this very night, is young Darby Riley going to be married to Bridget Rooney; and as she is a tall and comely girl, and has come of decent people, I think of marrying her myself, and taking her off with me.'

'And what will Darby Riley say to that?' said Billy.

'Silence!' said the little man, putting on a mighty severe look. 'I did not bring you here with me to ask questions.' Without holding further argument, he began saying the queer words, which had the power of passing him through the key-hole as free as air, and which Billy thought himself mighty clever to be able to say after him.

In they both went; and for the better viewing the company, the little man perched himself up as nimbly as a cock-sparrow upon one of the big beams which went across the house over all their heads, and Billy did the same upon another facing him; but not being much accustomed to roosting in such a place, his legs hung down as untidy as may be, and it was quite clear he had not taken pattern after the way in which the little man had bundled himself up together. If the little man had been a tailor all his life, he could not have sat more contentedly upon his haunches.

There they were, both master and man, looking down upon the fun that was going forward – and under them were the priest and piper – and the father of Darby Riley, with Darby's two brothers and his uncle's son – and there were both the father and the mother of Bridget Rooney, and proud enough the old couple were that night of their daughter, as good right they had – and her four sisters with brand new ribbons in their caps, and her three brothers all looking as clean and as clever as any three boys in Munster – and there were uncles and aunts, and gossips and cousins enough besides to make a full house of it – and plenty was there to eat and drink on the table of every one of them, if they had been double the number.

Now it happened, just as Mrs Rooney had helped his reverence to the first cut of the pig's head which was placed before her, beautifully bolstered up with white savoys, that the bride gave a sneeze which made every one at table start, but not a soul said 'God bless us'. All thinking that the priest would have done so, as he ought if he had done his duty, no one wished to take the word out of his mouth, which unfortunately was preoccupied with pig's head and greens. And after a moment's pause, the fun and merriment of the bridal feast went on without the pious benediction.

Of this circumstance both Billy and his master were not inattentive spectators from their exalted stations. 'Ha!' exclaimed the little man, throwing one leg from under him with a joyous flourish, and his eye twinkled with a strange light, whilst his eyebrows became elevated into the curvature of Gothic arches – 'Ha!' said he, leering down at the bride, and then up at Billy. 'I have half of her now, surely. Let her sneeze but twice more, and she is mine, in spite of priest, mass book, and Darby Riley.'

Again the fair Bridget sneezed; but it was so gently, and she blushed so much, that few except the little man took, or seemed to take, any notice; and no one thought of saying 'God bless us'.

Billy all this time regarded the poor girl with a most rueful expression of countenance; for he could not help thinking what a terrible thing it was for a nice young girl of nineteen, with large blue eyes, transparent skin, and dimpled cheeks, suffused with health and joy, to be obliged to marry an ugly little bit of a man, who was a thousand years old, barring a day.

At this critical moment the bride gave a third sneeze, and Billy roared out with all his might, 'God save us!'

Whether this exclamation resulted from his soliloquy, or from the mere force of habit, he never could tell exactly himself; but no sooner was it uttered, than the little man, his face glowing with rage and disappointment, sprung from the beam on which he had perched himself, and shrieking out in the shrill voice of a cracked bagpipe, 'I discharge you my service, Billy Mac Daniel – take that for your wages,' gave poor Billy a most furious kick in the back, which sent his unfortunate servant sprawling upon his face and hands right in the middle of the supper-table.

If Billy was astonished, how much more so was every one of the company into which he was thrown with so little ceremony: but when they heard his story, Father Cooney laid down his knife and fork, and married the young couple out of hand with all speed; and Billy Mac Daniel danced at their wedding, and plenty did he drink at it too, which was what he thought more of than dancing.

10: THE BIG MAN OF THE FAIRIES

SEUMAS O'KELLY*

... OUL' TOM KELLEHER was sitting with his back up against one of the cocks, fiddling with a súgán with a long rib of hay between his teeth ... When Padraic asked him if he'd tell them a story, oul' Tom looked hard at him for a good bit. It wasn't everyone Tom would give out a story to, but he liked to have little people about him ...

Oul' Tom Kelleher looked over the field, and the eyes of him rested on a fairy fort that you could see near the hedge, with its sides all covered with ferns, oul' ancient bushes growing in the middle of it, and a swamp around about it with a green growth upon it where even a frog would hardly venture if he was to get all the slugs in the world.

"Tisn't for me or for you,' said Tom Kelleher, 'to be puttin' the evil word on them that has the fort beyond, but if there is a man from here to Hong Kong and back that has cause to say the bad

---

* From *The Leprechaun of Killmeen* by Seumas O'Kelly.

word of them, I'm that same man. And I'll tell ye
how that is.

"'Twas a fine summer evening I was comin'
down along the road after a long walk in the heat of
the day when I sat up on the ditch against the
demesne wall down at the cross to ease me feet and
take a pull of the pipe. The light of day was falling
at the time, and I felt very drowsy in meself. I was
just beginning to nod when all of a sudden I saw a
little oul' man peeping out from behind a laurel
bush in the demesne, where the gap is in the wall.
The little oul' man wasn't the height of me knee,
and you never saw such a wizened oul' face as he
had on him. He was peepin' at me just the same as
if he was ready to make a bolt if I moved an inch;
but I never stirred or let on to see a trace of him.
Then, all of a sudden, I thought of who he was and
the heart began to wallop the sides out of me. May
the angels fly away with me if it wasn't the
Leprechaun himself that was in it.

'Faith, I tell you what, I wasn't long dozing
then! The crock of gold that I'd have if I could only
once lay hands on him began to swim before me
eyes, and, strange as it may seem, I thought I was
standin' by the shore of Loughrea, and that crocks
of gold were bobbin' up and down on the waves
thick as you'd see the stars of silver dancin' on the
water, and meself and I pullin' in the crocks as fast
as every wash of the waves sent them clattering up
on the rocks. Sure 'twas moidhered me head was
entirely.

'But it cleared after a bit, an' I bethought to

meself that the only chance I had of ever leaving a hand on the Leprechaun and makin' him land out his crock of gold was by pretending that 'twas asleep I was. You see, there's nothing so crafty as a Leprechaun, and the only chance you have with him is by being craftier again, and although it's meself that says it, Tom Kelleher wasn't behind the door when they were giving out the wits an' craft. It's a good many cross-roads I passed in me day.

'So with that I began to snore out of me, at first easy, but after a while so as you'd hear me a quarter of a mile down the road. And I put one of me hands, be the way of no harm, over me face, as if 'twas raving I was in me dreams, so as I could get a squint at the Leprechaun and what he was up to out through me fingers. For a good long bit he stayed peeping out from behind the laurel, with his wizened oul' face, and then he began to move out to the gap in the demesne wall, coming step by step as cautious as a cat over water. He stood on one of the stones of the wall for a good bit, looking up an' down the road, and it put the heart across in me when I thought some misfortunate wastrel or another might come trapesing down the road, frighten the jewel of a Leprechaun, and rob me of me fine crock of gold. 'Tis often a decent man lost his gold or his life be a misfortune of the like.

'Well, as luck would have it, the sorra soul was coming along the road, and all of a sudden the Leprechaun jumped down out of the stone, took one race across the road like a rabbit, climbed up on the ditch about five yards from where I was stretched, an' putting his wee arm about an oul' hawthorn bush, looked about him on every side to see was there any danger. Faith, when I saw the little legs working like lightning as the Leprechaun took across the road, I had as much as ever I could do to keep from giving a scorth of a laugh out of me. 'Twas only the thoughts of me crock of gold that made me keep it in. I kept up the snoring and the sleeping moryah, but I can tell you it was no joke to do that same. But, an' oul' dog for the hard road.

'After a list the Leprechaun began to come over to me on his tipsy-toes, and he ready to fly at the first stir. I could feel him comin' up along to me feet, but couldn't see him now. Then he moved up along until he came to me pockets, an' may I never taste another bite of the world's bread if he didn't begin to feel every one of me pockets with the little hand of him.

'"Well," says I to meself, "well," says I, "it's news to me that Leprechauns are day-light robbers, but sure," says I, "'twas easily known," says I, "that 'twasn't by honest means they came by the gold they have in their crocks. But," says I to meself, "but he's welcome to all the gold he'll get in Tom Kelleher's pockets," says I. An' I had as much as I could do to keep in another scorth of a laugh at the notion of gold in my pockets.

'Well, he searched every one o' me pockets, an' I was tryin' to make up me mind whether I'd make a drive to grab him and demand me crock, but knowin' he was so swift I said I'd bide me time until I could get his back turned to me.

'By degrees he came up around me head and down by me face, an' that I may be as dead as me aunt's husband if he didn't give me moustache a twirl of his hand passing down.

'"That's a fine whisker entirely Tom Kelleher has on him," says he to himself. "A couple of the hairs out of it would make mighty fine tackling," says he, "for me jauntin' car, that I yoke me squirrels an' me weasles to. They wouldn't be any the worse, though," he says, runnin' his thin little fingers along one of the ribs, "of a good washin' down in the stream of Killmeen, for this same dirty oul' Tom Kelleher," he says, "isn't by any manner o' means the cleanest no more than the decentest man in the parish, not to talk of his streel of a wife."

'Well, as I say, I passed many a cross-roads in me day, but never was I so sore set before. I could stand anything about myself, but when he put disparagement on herself, that is one of the finest housekeepers, and the tastiest woman that stands the country, I had every mind to jump up and squeeze the life out of the weeshy malafacthur. But, no; I kept me temper, for I knew 'twas all the craft of the Leprechaun, because I couldn't see him without opening me eyes, and if I opened me eyes he'd see them, even in through me fingers, he was standing that close to my face. Before I'd have them half opened he'd be off the ditch in a leap and my only chance was to get his back turned.

'With that the Leprechaun walked down a bit saying to himself, "He's a terrible baste entirely, the

lazy slob of an ownshaugh, the good-for-nothin'
Tom Kelleher. There isn't another man in Killmeen
that wouldn't be ashamed of his life to be lying
there asleep on the ditch this blessed and holy evening, and he snoring out of him as if he wanted to
pull down the skies on the top of the people. Sure,"
he says, says he, "it must be dead drunk the oul'
villain is."

'Well, this to a man that kept his pledge honest
for twenty-five year, come next Lady Day, was
hard to bear, and I don't know to this hour how I
ever put up with it.

'The Leprechaun then went to another pocket
and searched it. "The sorra ha'penny he has at all
on him," says he. "I suppose his streel of a wife,"
says he, "couldn't be trusting him with it or else he
drank it all, the murdering wastrel. Not," says he,
"but that he ought to have enough of money on
him. 'Tis well known," says he, "where the stockin'
full of gold that the widow Brady had stolen from
her went, and who robbed Kieran Connors coming
home from the fair when he found the decent man
the worse of a little drop. As the people says, Tom
Kelleher," he says, "would steal the cross off an ass'
back."

'Well, when I thought of what herself would
say an' what herself would do if she heard the like
of this of me I made one leap up and a drive at the
Leprechaun.

'"Be this and be that," says I, with a holy roar,
"what a villainous liar the daylight robber of a
Leprechaun is!"

'The Leprechaun let one squeal out of him, and I fell off the ditch into the field, bringing him down with me. 'Twas the mercy of heaven he didn't come under me or I'd have crushed him like a grain of corn on the grinding stone. I made a wild grab at him and caught him by the tail of his little green jacket as he was gathering himself together.

'"Take off me, Tom Kelleher," he says, struggling, and that I may never sin if he didn't try to slip off the jacket, so as to leave it in my hands and escape. But I grabbed him by one of the arms, and it wasn't no more than the thickness of a kippeen.

'"You're not so smart as you think, me crafty Leprechaun," says I, "and don't forget it's Tom Kelleher," says I, "that you have to deal with – Tom Kelleher," says I, "that has the best woman of a wife from here to Dublin town – Tom Kelleher," says I, "that always kept himself fine and decent and respectable – Tom Kelleher," says I, "that was never yet beholden for anyone to do his business for him – Tom Kelleher," says I, "that has his pledge close on five-and-twenty good years – Tom Kelleher," says I, "that never begged, borr'd, or stole from man, woman, or child his life's len'th," says I. "And," says I, "you'll be just showing me where that crock of gold of mine is, an' no more of your Andra Martins."

'The Leprechaun got fine and quiet then, and made no more attempt to get away. He just let a sigh out of him. "Let out of me arm, Tom," he says. "I'm caught now and the crock of gold is yours," he says. "All you need do," says he, "is to keep your eye on me until I show you where it's buried. It's surprising to me," he says, "that you don't know that much."

'Well, I let out of him, but kept me two eyes on him, and he sat down on a stone. He examined his little jacket, and says, "Musha, Tom," says he, "you nearly tore the coat off me. And what harm, but it took a thousand of the best ants in the parish," he says, "six months to spin and weave that same coat, and two thousand more of them to pick the wool for it off the lambs an' dye it green with the herbs. The trimming," says he, "is of the best of flaggers and they frilled." His little breeches were made out of white ceannabhain, plucked below in the bog and spun by the ants. He said the Bean Sidhe washed and beetled them for him once a week below in the stream, and they were certainly fine and white. His boots were made by the Cluricaun from bullrushes, laced with fairy-flax, and his cap was a dried mushroom, covered with the copper-coloured leaves of a beech tree, that the Pooka made him a present of last Samhain Night. But 'twas the little old wizened face of him with all the wrinkles on it, that was the wonder of the world to see. He put one leg over his knee as he sat on the stone and that was the comical cut he made of it. He was the drollest sight you ever saw.

'But I wanted my crock of gold an' all the time I was thinking of all I'd do with it. I'd have the finest place in Killmeen and make a queen of herself – what she was well fit for.

'"Hurry on," says I, "and show me where my

crock of gold is."

'"Oh," says the Leprechaun, "you needn't fret about your gold. If you were as sure of getting heaven, you'd be all right. But be easy for a bit. Sure, I'm so dying for a talk and a smoke, Tom. It's forty years since I was caught before, and the man that caught me then didn't grudge me a bit of t'baccy."

'Well, I couldn't do less than hand him a bit of t'baccy that was ground up nice and fine. He put his hand in his breeches' pocket and took out the half of a nutshell, stuck a bit of kippeen in a little hole that was in it, filled in the t'baccy, struck a match and pulled away as happy as you please.

'"Musha, Tom," says he, "this is the grand smoke entirely. If you hadn't a pull out of your pipe for forty years, 'tis you that'd relish it."

'"Meaning no insult," says I, "you must be very old."

'"I am, Tom," says he. "I'm as old as the hills of Connemara." And he pulled away at his pipe, looking down very thoughtful-like all the time. I kept my eyes well on him, for you couldn't be up to the craft of the like of him.

'"When all is said and done," says he, all of a sudden, without looking up, "she was a mean oul' rip."

'"Who was?" says I.

'"Herself," says he.

'"Oh," says I, "I didn't know there was a Mrs Leprechaun. Long life to her," says I.

'"No," says he, "there was no Mrs Leprechaun,

only there very nearly was. That's how the whole row rose," says he.

"'Musha, do you tell me so?" says I.

"'I do, in throth," says he.

"'Glory be to God," says I.

"'Herself," says he, taking another pull, "was the Queen of the Fairies. A fine woman, no doubt, Tom, but a bit ould and stale. But her daughter, the Princess, was a fine young woman, and no mistake. She wasn't more than a couple of thousand year in them days, and she looking as sweet and as fresh as the daisy that puts its head up over the green sod in the spring."

"'The craythur," says I.

'The Leprechaun shook his head sadly, and blew a pull of the pipe out of his mouth. "Me heart," says he, "was broke after her."

"'God help us!" says I.

"'Tom Kelleher!" says he, jumpin' up an' stickin' out his bit of a chest, "I'd have it be known to you," he says, "that I was the *Fear Mor* (Big Man) of the Fairies!"

"'Thunder and turf, you were," says I.

"'I was," says he. "Finn Mac Cumhail," says he, "couldn't hold a candle to me. An'," says he, "I sought the hand of the daughter o' the Queen an' there was a great gradh on her for me. But the oul' strap of a mother wouldn't hear tell of it. Instead, what does she do," says he, "but banish me from being the *Fear Mor* of Tir na nOg to be a Leprechaun on the world. She did it with a wave of her wand, the mean oul' streel."

'"Meelia murdher," says I.

'"An," says he, "she put a curse upon me an' I goin'. The curse was that I should go around takin' all the gold I could get an' puttin' it into crocks, an' when I had crocks o' gold hid away that'd be as high as Croagh Patrick, when they'd be dug up that I'd get back to Tir na nOg an' be the *Fear Mor* o' the Fairies again."'

'"Croagh Patrick is a nice little bit of hill," says I.

'"Tis," says he; "and to make it worse, the oul' strap sent me into the hardest country in the world to get gold from the people in. But," says he, "if any man laid a hand on me an' then kep' his eye on me I'd have to give him out the last crock o' gold I buried."

'"The jewel of a Queen," says I, keepin' me eyes on the Leprechaun.

'"But," says he, "if I could get away from him or get his eye off me I need give him no crock, an' the Fairies would bury a hundred crocks for me," he says.

'"The sorra hundred crocks I'll be the means of givin' ye," says I.

'"An'," says he, givn' another sigh out of him, "the poor little child of a Princess is waitin' for me to come back to wed her."

'"The tinder chicken of the world," says I.

'"Ochone!" says he.

'"Mo bhron!" says I.

'"The last crock I buried," says he, "is –"

'"Where?" says I.

79

'"Come on and I'll show you," says he, "you heartless oul' varmint." An' with that he knocked out the ashes out of his nut-shell on the heel of his bullrush shoe, pressed down the t'baccy with his fingers, and put it in his pocket an' stood up.

'"Hurry on," says I.

'"You haven't far to go," says he.

'"So best," says I.

'"An' may it melt with you," says he, "an' your seven generations after you."

'"A fine thing to have to melt it is," says I; "hurry on me *Fear Mor* of the Fairies."

'"Keep your eye on me," says he.

'"I wouldn't look at you if it was to save me life," says I, an' I glued my eyes on him.

'He walked down the fields an' I after him, an' to see him steppin' out with the little legs of him an' you'd never do a day's good. An' all the time I was plannin' in me head what I'd buy an' what I'd get when I had me lashin's of gold. I'd show Killmeen what it never saw before.

'Well, where did he bring me but right into the meadow here, where the aftergrass was growin'. He headed along up the meadow, an' as we came along I heard a footstep behind us. I was dyin' to know who was in it, but couldn't look back.

'"Hould on," says I, "there's someone behind us an' he'll see us," says I.

'"What harm," says he.

'"'Tis ," says I, "for you'll have to give him another crock o' gold if he nabs you."

'"A crock here or there," said he, "when you

80

come to think of the size o' Croagh Patrick, won't make much odds."

'"But," says I, "'tis many a long day you'll be collectin' the filling' of a crock in Killmeen."

'"I'm a long liver," says he.

'"An' the poor Princess," says I, "she'll be wasted entirely waitin' for you."

'"She's only a child," says he, "an' we'll give her time to grow."

'The footsteps were comin' nearer to us all the time, an' I was cursin' whoever was in it.

'"Can't you wait a minute," says I, "an' he'll pass?"

'"You're in a hurry, you said," says he.

'"I'm not, now," says I.

'"But I am," says he. "It's Martin Moran," says he, "that's in it."

'Well, when I heard that I nearly dropped. Martin Moran an' me weren't the best of friends, an' it was givin' up to him that a meaner or more graspin' or a hungrier hound didn't stand in the country. I'd as soon meet the divil as Martin Moran, an' I havin' the Leprechaun.

'"I'll have to be houldin' you by mean force," says I, "if you don't stand for a bit."

'"Musha," says he, steppin' out, an' his legs seemed to be gettin' longer an' longer every inch of the way, "is it begrudgin' one of the neighbours a crock of gold ye are? An' you are the dacent, sober man, Tom Kelleher," he says, "that never did a wrong turn!"

'I made a dive at the Leprechaun an' he took to

the Galtees like a hare an' I after him.

'"Oh, meelia murdher! it's a Leprechaun," says the voice of Martin Moran, an' with that he took after the Leprechaun, too. I could hear him, an' partly see him as he took along the meadow, but I made sure to keep me eyes on the Leprechaun.

'"He's my Leprechaun, Martin Moran," I called out, "an' you have no business to be after him." I felt ragin' mad with the hungry hound.

'"He's belongin' to whoever catches him," Moran shouted back. The Leprechaun used to look back over his shoulder an' he runnin', an' I knew by the way he was manoeuvrin' that he wanted to get Martin Moran between mesel' an' the line of sight so that the spell would be broken. There's no beatin' the craft of a Leprechaun, an' there he was, turnin' an' twistin' for all the world like a hare an' we turnin' him here an' there like a pair of hounds over the meadow. The aftergrass was thick an' high an' I knew that by all the turnin' an' twistin' that the Leprechaun thought I'd trip an' fall, an' then, of course, I'd have to take me eyes off him.

'I never thought that an' oul' man could run the way Martin Moran ran that evenin' after the Leprechaun in the meadow.

'"Crocks o' goold! Crocks o' goold!" Martin roared out of him, an' he made a spurt the same as if he had a pair of wings. He got into the Leprechaun in a couple of bounds, an' the next I saw was the two of them rollin' over in the grass.

'"Crocks o' goold, yer soul!" cried Martin.

'"He's mine, I tell ye," I roared, an' fell in a

heap down on the two of them. Martin had the Leprechaun by one of the legs an' I grabbed a hold of the other one.

'"I had him first," Martin cried, gettin' up on his knees, holdin' his leg. "Not by any manner o' means, Martin," says I. "I had him above on the ditch, an' we were only comin' down for the crock when you happened to come across us. Let go o' me Leprechaun."

'"Misfortune to Killmeen, anyhow," says the Leprechaun, "an' the first day I ever put a foot in it. It's murdhered I'll be entirely with them."

'"Don't be killin' the craythur," says I.

'"It's yoursel' that's on for killin' him," says Martin.

'"Ye're both killin' me dead," says the Leprechaun. "It'll be another case o' killin' the goose with the golden eggs."

'"Faith, an' it won't," says Martin, "if Tom Kelleher has some sort of reason in him."

'"All right, let go of your leg, an' I'll let go of mine, an' we'll leave it to the Leprechaun," says I. "After all, 'tis him that has the gold," says I. "An' let him say who's entitled to it."

'"Keep ye're eyes on me," says the Leprechaun, "but let go of my legs."

'We let go his legs, an' kept our eyes on him. The Leprechaun sat up, an' pulled a rib of the aftergrass, wipin' his face with it. He sighed a great, long sigh. "I won't be the better o' this," he says, "for the next fifty year."

'"Give out the crock you were bringin' me for,"

says I, "an' no more of your antics."

"'But you'll be pleased to hand me over mine first, as I caught you first," says Martin Moran.

'The Leprechaun sighed again. "Killmeen will be the fine rich place shortly," says he.

"'There'll be them that'll be well off in it, anyhow," says Martin Moran, an' I knew the hungry eyes were blazin' with greed in his head.

"'They'll be rollin' in riches in Killmeen," says the Leprechaun, settlin' the mushroom of a hat on him.

"'Martin Moran?" says I, starin' at the Leprechaun, "this carractan of a Leprechaun is only killin' time to make up in his crafty oul' head how he'll get away from us. If he gives both of us the slip, he'll have two hundred crocks of gold buried for him by the fairies."

"'He'll never leave my sight," says Martin Moran, "so long as there's an eye in my head."

"'One poor little Leprechaun agin two big men from the parish o' Killmeen!" says the Leprechaun, with another sigh. "It's the world that's badly matched anyhow."

"'An', Martin Moran," says I, "if you have any dacency or spirit in ye, ye won't be goin' between me an' my crock, that I earned honest above at the ditch, before ever you dreamt there was a Leprechaun in the parish."

"'We'll hear about that some other time," says Martin. "Why didn't you hold him when you had him, if what you say is true, which I don't feel inclined to b'lieve."

'That Martin Moran is a terrible hound, an' no mistake. I was mad enough to take him by the throttle, only I knew if I did I'd lose my crock.

'"The neighbours," says the Leprechaun, fixing one of his bullrush shoes, that got loose from the struggle, "will be wonderin' where all the grandeur an' all the riches an' all the high notions came from. They won't hear much about the *Fear Mor* of the Fairies," he says, lookin' up at me with a sharp oul' eye, an' the head of him cocked to one side. "Will they, Tom a leanbh?" he says.

'"Give out the crock o' gold," says I, ragin', "that you were bringin' me for, if you're an honest Leprechaun."

'"I'm all that," says he.

'"But you'll be landin' out mine first," says Martin Moran.

'"Bedad, anyhow," says the Leprechaun, "it's Killmeen that's goin' to flourish."

'I jumped up, keepin' me eyes on him. Martin Moran jumped up, too. I walked over an' took the Leprechaun by the arm an' shook him. "My crock of gold, quick," says I.

'Martin Moran shook the other arm. "After me," says he.

'The Leprechaun looked up at us with his oul' face. '"Kilmeen," says he, "will be rotten with money, an' we'll be givin' big fortunes to all the daughters."

'I shook him again an' Martin shook his side.

'"We'll have sprees an' parties an' ructions of all kinds," says the Leprechaun. "Them that hadn't a decent wheelbarrow," he says, "will be goin' in for a carriage an' pair."

'I gave him a better shake, an' Martin did the same.

'"My crock," says I.

'"My crock," says Martin.

'"An' some of us, maybe, will be goin' in for a footman," says the Leprechaun. "We'll be knockin' th' oul' house with the rain down," says he, "an' buildin' palaces. An' we'll have the quality drivin' up to us."

'"That'll do, now," says I.

'"The crock, like a decent man," says Martin.

'"The wonders of the world," says he, "will be comin' over Killmeen. The stream will be runnin' red with wine."

'Faith we both began shakin' him like the dickens, an' he got up on his legs an' began to struggle with us.

'"Is it murder ye're on for?" he says, shoulderin' here an' there.

'"Not at all," says I. "It's only that crock of gold of mine you were bringing me for we want."

'"Just my crock," says Martin, "and then yourself and Tom Kelleher can talk it out about the other one," he says, "the grabber."

'"Take o' me," says the Leprechaun, "or the sorra crock ye'll ever see. Keep ye're hungry oul' eyes on me, but don't be tearin' the clothes off me back. Misfortune to Killmeen, anyhow."

'We let out of him then and kept our eyes on him instead. He stood out from us, put his two thumbs in the armpits of his waistcoat, struck his two legs well apart, and putting the head of him to one side, looked up at us with his oul' face. "To business, gentlemen," says he, like any lawyer in a courthouse, "to business. This is how the land lies, my good friends. We want two crocks of gold. Very well. One crock there lies buried under the oul' bush in –"

'"Where?" we both cried, holding our breath, as the Leprechaun paused.

'The Leprechaun put his head over to the other side and grinned up at us. "In the neighbourhood," he says, with a sweep of his wee hand that took in nine parishes.

'"That's the last one I buried. The one I buried before that is above in –"

'Again the Leprechaun paused, an' we both asked, "Where?" with our hearts in our mouths waitin' the wink of the word.

'"In Donegal," says the Leprechaun.

'You can be goin' away up to Donegal with the Leprechaun, Tom," says Martin Moran to me.

'"Thank you, Martin," says I, "but 'twould be well worth your own while to be thinkin' o' makin' the journey yoursel'. 'Tisn't everyone that gets a crock o' gold for goin' to Donegal, an' mesel' an' the Leprechaun were comin' for the one under the oul' bush when we came across you."

'"It seems, gentlemen," says the Leprechaun, "that we can't agree an' the night is comin' on. I'll tell you what we'll do. We'll have a short race for it. I'll go first, ten yards ahead of ye. Keep ye're eyes on me. I can't run so fast as I'd get out o' ye're sight. But whichever one of ye gets to the fort above first will get the first crock. The other one will get the one above in Donegal. Done!" he says.

'Neither mysel' or Martin Moran relished this, an' we began to object, but the Leprechaun moved back a couple of steps while we were arguin'. We'd have struck each other only that we knew if we did we'd lose the gold. I was foamin' an' Martin Moran was tearin'. All of a sudden, the Leprechaun shouts, "One, two, three, an' away!" an' off with him towards the fort.

'It was a good way up. Martin an' myself kep' up to each other an' our eyes on the Leprechaun. He went only middlin' fast, an' we kep' fairly well on to him. By reason of having to keep our eyes on him we stumbled an' staggered a great deal. Martin Moran began to work his arms an' his elbows to keep me back, an' I did the same to him. We were for all the world like a pair of madmen tearin' up the meadow, an' as we came nearer the fort we were shovin' an' jostlin' each other an' shoutin' an' tellin' each other what we thought about each other's seven generations. 'Twas a wonder of the world we didn't bring all in the parish down about us. A couple of times when Martin staggered I was dead sure he was done for, but he'd lie into me in a minute again, an' he shoutin', "I've me eye on him". An' I was nearly gone a couple of other times, but I kep' me eye on the Leprechaun, an' mighty hard I found it to get into Martin again. How an oul' man like him ran that mortal day beat out everything else. Glory be to God! but 'twas wonderful.

'As we came up to the fort the oul' Leprechaun gained on us, an' the legs of him seemed to be len'thenin' out. He looked back at us. "Keep ye're eyes on me whatever ye do," he'd call back. "Keep them on me! Gold in crocks yer soul!"

'Well, I think the eyes were burstin' out of our heads, as we went flyin', an' stumblin', and shovin', an' pushin', an' shoulderin' along. As we came up to the fort, both the one an' the other of us was blowin' like whales, an' we made one desperate, gaspin' spurt. "Death or glory," says the Leprechaun, an' we threw out our arms before us. We were goin' neck an' neck. "Gold in crocks!" shouted the Leprechaun. "Tom Kelleher for ever!" he yelled. "Martin Moran, me life on ye!"

'Martin put one of his arms all of a sudden around me neck. He was gettin' weak; an' thought I'd go from him, but sure, what with the runnin' an' the excitement, I was as weak as a cat mesel', so I put my arm around Martin's neck. We staggered on this way, one not able to let the other go. The Leprechaun was now goin' like a rabbit on its track into a burrow. "Death or glory!" he shouted. I made one last dyin' plunge, for I thought Martin was beat up. Martin made another dyin' plunge. We weren't a hen's race from the fort. We had had our eyes as fast on the Leprechaun as a setter on a grouse in the heather, an' the two of us, gaspin' for life, staggerin', tremblin' all over an' I thought I could see oceans of gold before me. As we had our

eyes on the Leprechaun we couldn't rightly see
what was before us. The Leprechaun made a spring
up on the fort, an' began to dance for joy on one
leg, and then on the other, an' takin' off his mushroom cap, began to wave it at us. "Me soul for
ever," he cried, "Glory! Sorra such a race was ever
seen in nineteen baronies. Tom, ye jewel, your last
gasp! Martin, me son, a dyin' skip! Now for it. Take
the pool, me hearties!"

'Well, we never thought of the pool. We gave a
sort of a stagger for it, then the legs went clean, and
decent from under us an' as we went down, an'
knew all was up, an' that each of us had done the
other out of our gold for ever, we locked in each
other's arms. I think Martin Moran made an offer to
kiss me, an' as well as I remember, I gave him a
last, lovin' hug to me scalded heart.

'The last thing I heard was a laugh up in the
fort.

'"Two hundred crocks!" I heard the Leprechaun shoutin' "Croagh Patrick is comin' down!"

'Then I felt smotherin' an' gurglin' an' suffo-
catin', an' struggled out of Martin's lovin' em-
brace. I made one leap in the water – an' found
meself sittin' up, shiverin' with the cold, on the
ditch over the demesne wall.

'There wasn't a sound in the place only the
shakin' of the leaves of the laurel tree near the gap
...'

A History of Irish Fairies

Carolyn White

Whether you believe in fairies or not, you cannot ignore them, and here for the first time is *A History of Irish Fairies*. Having no stories directly from the fairies themselves, we must rely on descriptions by mortal men and women. A large part of the book is concerned with the relations between mortals and fairies, so that the reader may determine the best way to behave whenever he encounters fairies. You can read about the Far Darrig, Merrows and Silkies, Banshees and Keening, the Lianhan Shee, Pookas, Dullahans and Ghosts.

Superstitions of the Irish Country People

Padraic O'Farrell

Irish country people believed that fairies were always present among them and that around the next corner or in the very next clump of thistles there might well be somebody lurking who would lead them to the crock of gold at the end of the rainbow. Fairies were good to mortals who observed the superstitions which called for leaving them food, not throwing out water without first shouting a warning on them, and so on.

Irish Fairy Tales

Michael Scott

'He found he was staring directly at a leprechaun. The small man was sitting on a little mound of earth beneath the shade of a weeping willow tree ... the young man could feel his heart beginning to pound. He had seen leprechauns a few times before but only from a distance. They were very hard to catch, but if you managed at all to get hold of one ...'

Irish Animal Tales

Michael Scott

Have you ever noticed how cats and dogs sometimes sit up and look at something that is not there? Have you ever seen a dog barking at nothing? And have you ever wondered why?

Perhaps it is because the animal can see the fairy folk coming and going all the time, while humans can only see the Little People at certain times. The fairy folk often do favours for cats and dogs, and help them whenever they can.

Irish Hero Tales

Michael Scott

When we think of heroes we think of brave knights on horseback, wearing armour and carrying spears and swords. They do battle with demons and dragons, evil knights and magicians. But there are other kinds of heroes: heroes we never hear about.

Irish Folk Stories for Children

T Crofton Croker

These exciting and spell-binding stories are full of magical people and enchanted places which will delight and entertain children of all ages. *Irish Folk Stories for Children* are tales of past centuries when magic and mystery were part of everyone's life. They include such well-loved stories as 'The Giant's Stairs', 'The Legend of Bottle-Hill' and 'Soul Cages'.

Irish Lore and Legends

Selected and Edited by S M W Dunnit

Irish Lore and Legends is a beautifully illustrated collection of traditional Irish legends and folklore. The stories are based on the work of T W Rolleston, A P Graves, W B Yeats and T Crofton Croker and are an example of the richness of our Irish heritage and culture.

Among the stories included are 'A Legend of Knockmany', 'Diarmid Bawn, the Piper', 'The Hillman and the Housewife', 'The Haunted Cellar', 'The Demon Cat', 'The Black Hole of Knockfierna', 'Conan mac Morna', 'The Great Mr Barry of Cairn Thierna', 'Táin Bó Cuailgne' and 'The Voyage of Maeldún'.

'Before the Devil Knows You're Dead'
Irish Blessings, Toasts and Curses

Padraic O'Farrell

'May you be in heaven an hour before the devil knows you're dead.'

'May today be the first day of the best years of your life.'

'May the wind always be at your back.'

Hearing news of a death or marriage, consoling neighbours in sorrow or sharing their joy, looking for a husband or wife, saving turf or going fishing – Irish people had blessings and curses for every occasion. Luckily many of these sayings have survived. A few startling new ones have been added too!

The Wasp in the Mug

Gabriel Rosenstock

The wit and wisdom of the Gael are tightly packed in the Irish proverb.

> Is sleamhain an lao nach lifidh a mháthair fín í.
> Slippery is the calf that its own mother won't lick!

The Wasp in the Mug is a generous selection of old Irish proverbs like these, newly translated from the Irish by Gabriel Rosenstock, the most prolific poet and translator of his generation. He invites us to savour this collection as a bag of liquorice allsorts – to be dipped into and enjoyed when we feel the urge. But remember: 'Don't keep them all to yourselves. They're for sharing ...!'

Irish Proverbs and Sayings
Gems of Irish Wisdom

Padraic O'Farrell

Gems of Irish Wisdom is a fascinating collection of Irish proverbs and sayings.

The tallest flowers hide the strongest nettles.

The man who asks what good is money has already paid for his plot.

A man begins cutting his wisdom teeth the first time he bites off more than he can chew.

Even if you are on the right track, you'll be run over if you stay here.

The road to Heaven is well signposted but badly lit at night.

Love is like a stirabout. It must be made fresh today.

An Irish Almanac

Aidan Crealey

An Irish Almanac presents Irish history – political, social, economic and cultural – on an 'On this Day' basis, along with a comprehensive list of forth-coming centenaries (1994-2003).

Included here is information and commentary on notable personalities and events in Irish political history from the Battle of Clontarf (April 1014) to the Maastricht Referendum of June 1992, as well as extensive coverage of other aspects of Irish society, including literature and scholarship, music and the arts.

An Irish Almanac is the ideal companion for the armchair historian, quiz-master, tourist, racon-teur, student, speechmaker or indeed for anyone interested in the rich and varied world of Irish history.

The Irish Cookbook

Carla Blake

The Irish Cookbook fills a long felt need for a sound but attractive Cookbook for the young Irishwoman and every woman who would like to add to her culinary skills and try cooking Irish style.

Traditional Irish dishes are slightly adapted to suit present day tastes and methods and included are some modern Irish recipes using Guinness, Irish Whiskey, Irish hams and Irish cheese.

All the basic methods for making soup and cooking fish, meat and vegetables are given with a selection of unusual recipes. Suggestions are also made about accompaniments to make a pleasantly balanced meal. There are recipes to see you through all occasions from family meals and 'Quick and Easy' snacks to dinner parties.

The Irish Microwave Cookbook

Ann Ward

The Irish Microwave Cookbook contains Irish and international recipes for use in the most practical of homes. The recipes include everything from Irish stew to Lasagne and prove that there is no need for the purchase of special ingredients to be able to make full use of your microwave.